Pan Dulce for the Latinx Soul

Stories to Open the Heart and Heal the Soul

by
Sinai Cota

D1738160

Pan Dulce for the Latinx Soul,
Poems by Sinai Cota

Published by Sinai Cota

ISBN: 9798465903967

This book is dedicated to the families of Barrio Logan, and the *Kumeyaay* land I was raised on.

Dear Readers,

Thank you for purchasing Pan Dulce for the Latinx Soul. 100% of profits from this book will go towards funding college scholarships for first generation college students from under resourced communities through the Barrio Logan College Institute (San Diego, CA).

In the upcoming pages, I share my experiences about what it was like growing up in-between… straddling borders and managing my identities in Español, English, and Spanglish. I highlight topics that are often taboo and un-talked about in Latino/a/x culture.

My hope is that you read these poems and start a dialogue within yourself and your families. Think about your role and contributions to your community and those in need. Challenge authority and tradition, recognize your biases on gender, sexuality, skin color and the Black Lives Matter Movement. The Chicano/a/x identity was inspired in working with the Black Power movement, in an extremely tense social and political time experienced by Mexican-Americans in the 1960's. Chicano/a/x was born by and for the people by El Movimiento (The Movement) to fight for equality.

Your race, gender and culture, are assets to help you eradicate injustice in this world. Channel your ancestors and search for opportunities to engage in meaningful change. I've included 30 journaling prompts at the end of the book to help you reflect. And some coloring pages just for fun and to help you de-stress! Listen, never forget where your strength comes from. Learn to rest not quit. And remember, you are made of magic.

Con mucho cariño (with love), enjoy!

Sinai Cota

IG: Pink Chicana Poet

Table of Contents: La Panaderia

Pan Dulce Poems

Prompts to Help You Process

Pink Chicana Poet's Coloring Book

Pan Dulce

Soy pan dulce.
A sublime experience with
each mouthful.

Que delicia. Saboreame.
Soy cultura, amor y tradición.

No te empalago.
Soy justo lo que ocupa tu paladar.

Baked to perfection under the sun.
Pink and brown curves that wrap
around fluffy edges of mi
corazón.

I'm exactly what you've been
craving.

De Colores

Ni de aquí ni de allá.
De colores.
Somewhere in-between.
Unbound and Magical.

The blindfold is off and I'm discovering labels
that I never knew were possible.

Hay una fiesta dentro de mi lista para mi llegagda
Una celebracion, un poco tarde, pero al fin aquí estoy!

Here and Queer.

Cómo la piñata ✳ vibrante y llena de dulzura.
Soy la alegría que sientes cuando miras los dulces
caer.

Bolsitas of love are handed out as reminders that we
are a variety of delicious take-aways to be
celebrated every day.

Barrio Logan

Tucked away under the Coronado bridge -
there's a vibrant Mexican community filled with the
sweet smells of pan dulce.

Pink conchitas from Panchita's bakery and nieve from
Tocumbo in my cup.

Around the corner Las Cuatro Milpas feeds the
community home-made love wrapped in tortillas.

The ocean, nearby, manifests a calm and serene
breeze.

It's home…

Danzantes fill the park center, chanting by the
grandiosity of our murals that tell a story of our
struggles and triumphs.

The wind carries the drumming sounds through our
community, fighting to keep our culture alive.

Noches en Resistencia/ (*Nights in resistance*)

Balazos despegan como cohetes / (*Bullets fly up like fireworks*)

Powerful and abrupt.

The sirens wail like La Llorona looking for brown children ready to take them away.

Meanwhile the seeds under the bridge begin to sprout out from the ground fiercely taking their place.

We are the trees, with deep roots in the earth that you tried to cut down

Pero aquí seguimos, plumas en la cabeza y cascabeles en los tobillos,

Bailando hasta la gloria/ (*Dancing until our glory*). We are Chicanas/os/xs de Aztlán.

A Chicana in Wonderland

Like Alice in Wonderland I was ready for an
adventure. I ate the cookie, and learned to shrink
from place to place between the dark corners of
Logan and Tijuana.

Until a fat cat greeted me and riddled me out into a
garden of another world. Just across the border of
daisies. A tea party was happening and the white
rabbit was waiting unaware of my journey and the
dents under my fingers from holding onto dreams
that felt like they'd never become real, until I could
find my way back home.

You're late, he said!

The red queen waddled out from the nopales and
asked: "Where are you going? and Where do
you come from?" And like a Chicana true and true, le
dije: "Vengo de Aztlan de aqui y de alla."

Then I ate the nopal and did what I did best, shrunk
to survive…waiting to find my way back again.

La Migra (ICE/Border Patrol)

They scrape the humanity out of you like gutting a
pumpkin on Halloween night.

Grin over you, a hollow shell they've proudly created
and eagerly showcase you to the world.

They fill your insides with spooky stories of *bad
hombres* before sending you off trick-or-treating
through the Mexican neighborhoods, with a
machete in hand, ready to cut down abuelitas and
babies, like Jason.

YOU are a living-breathing- horror story–ready to
deport their bodies, hopes, and dreams because it's
your job.

You watch unfazed as my 4ft mom is handcuffed-
deemed a criminal and arrested, for cleaning your
toilets, washing your clothes and scrubbing your
floors- - a job most Americans won't dare to do.

In an instant, she is discarded into a country she no longer calls home, displaced and confused, while you return back...safe...to your family to eat dulces.

Your bellies are full of kit-kats and skittles while...my family is consumed by a nightmare: crying in cages under foil blankets for a chance to live.

I bury myself deep into the ground hiding: alone, homeless and hungry; hoping for the sun's warm embrace and a new day to find me beneath the dirt.

I go undetected to the rest of the world–a slumbering cocoon nourished by the soil ready to be born again.

I take a deep breath and sprout wings on my back flying up to the clouds.

I am home. I am safe. And I am everything I've hoped for.

Malinche

I am the Malinche. Traitor and slave.

I grew up in a world where my dad thought it was okay to kidnap me, just like Hérnan Cortez, the Spanish Conquistador, had done so many years ago–to the Nahua girl: Malinche.

He showed up to the gates of my school ready to lay claim to me, like I was the Aztec Empire. With one hand on my back and another on my arm, he guided me in a forceful-fast pace out of my elementary school and to his car.

My mom and principal rescued me from his grip, but not from this world, where more men thought they could occupy my body; where I thought I had to destroy the brown inside me: cut it down, deny it, burn it- to stay alive.

I grew up in a world where I hid myself within the white crowds, praying to fit in just to survive.

I took advantage of my fair skin, courtesy of the colonizers to hide among the gringos.

I sacrificed my culture and family to earn a place in this world, along Hérnan Cortez and the other conquistadors where my captors convinced me: clean water and paved roads would keep me safe. But I am not safe.

And while I am alive, in the here and now, I know safety will come from the other Malinches. I will search to find them and take back our world making it safe for all of us to be in...

I am the Malinche. Survivor and brave.

Frida

Me cubro en tu imagen como si fueras Santa.
Rezo con el pincel entre mis dedos.
Y cuando corre el miedo tras mi espalda, busco tu
imagen que me ofrece protección;
Y en ese momento… sé que no estoy sola.

Cuando pinto, guías mi mano para descubrir un lugar
fuera del alcance del mundo corrupto y perverso
del hombre.

Y ahí estás tú.
De colores, lo que me libera mi alma
y me llena de luz.

Y tocan mi piel bautizándome
una pintora, poeta, y mujer.

Pero el amor, cariño, y orgullo que llevo dentro
desaparecen en un instante cuando ellos me dicen
que no soy lo suficiente.

Pero entre lo oscuro de tus artes encuentro claridad y
el esfuerzo para seguir adelante.

Me invitas a crear mi propio realidad.

En medio de tus cejas
Encurentro una sonrisa.
.
Viva la Frida.

Pocha

My mouth rejoices when it exhales the sweet
intertwined words of:
"Hola, qué tal and nice to meet you", a sigh of relief
when they can understand both.

This is what it means to be Chicana, but they call you
Pocha, like you're less than, incomplete.
But I am whole, living in the in-between.

Chicana means community. Power. Courage.

My brain acknowledges Spanglish as a real language.
But the world sees it as broken, and prompts me to
pick a side.

Pocha or Beaner. It's a war and
there isn't room for both.

Like Selena's dad says: "You gotta be more Mexican
than the Mexicans and more American than the
Americans!"

Why can't I exist in both?

I'm still a Mexicana, even if I eat frijoles from a can, or
don't speak Spanish well. And I'm American, not
just because I'm born in San Diego, but I played
sports and celebrate the 4th, soy Americana.

Tortillas hechas a mano or from the Hispanic aisle at
Ralphs. Soy Mexicana.
There is room for both in my belly.
I'm living and breathing proof we can co-exist.
It's been done.

Here I am.
Aquí estoy y no me voy.

Amigas & Wine

I fill my house with wine instead of friends.
Because my grandma told me not to trust women.

Me dijo:
Women betray you
Women backstab you
Mujeres son envidiosas
Mujeres son puro drama

So I drink alone finding company in my poems.
Thinking of community.
Dreaming of amigas to toast my cup with.

Un brindis a las mujeres que me
han enseñado una amistad sincera.

Cheers to the women who rallied around me
when I published my book.

To the women who answered my texts when I had no
one else.

To the women who traveled with me
and protected me.

To the mujeres who prove my grandmother wrong
each time we hang out.

The femme fatal.
La tomboy.
La chingona.

Bailamos?

Listen…the way the sounds wake up
the beats inside you like a sprinkler
watering confidence into your body.

Careless. And fierce. A magical force.
Generating light and energy.

People fall in love with your shape and the way it
bends and twirls.

Evolving, thriving and taking what's yours.
Space.

The dance floor is home.

You lead because you know exactly
where you're going.

Music birthed you and it saves you
from the pain when you break.

It welcomes you back each time, taking you to the
depths of your unexplored self.

Somos danzantes connected to the earth.
Falling in love with each other.

Opening up our spirits to the universe.

Black boots on our feet and flowers on our heads.

Elvis Crespo's suavemente at a quince or at that
corner bar, resurrects a familiar feeling.

Bailamos?

Calaveras y Muertos

I lit the calavera candles and said your name.
Papel picado, incense and sage.
From the world of the dead to the living.
I sing you a prayer, a hymn.
As the candles dim.
Memories alive give the spirit a chance to thrive.
I call to you for strength and wisdom
And welcome you back knowing it will all be fine.
Please come for one more night
where our souls can dine.
Sweet bread and wine.
Together comemos un pan de muerto.
Mientras la catrina baila y la cena comienza.
Tonight there is no pain or heartache,
rejoice and eat some cake!
Here comes our family, loved ones, and more.
To dance and feast by the marigolds.
Lurking beneath that shadow.
No need to fear the darkness.
Look! The sky's and stars aglow,
giving us all a fun show.
Soon a kiss and hug to say goodbye it's time to let go…

Si Se Puede

I see my dad in my classmate, a former inmate –
trying to better himself and his community.
I try to encourage him more.

I see my mother in the janitors, housekeepers, and
maids at hotels – working hard and with big
smiles. I try to tip them more.

I see my abuela in the street vendors always hustling,
I always buy from them, share their business, and
write a review.

I see my tios in those struggling with addictions and
mental health and never seeking help-
I don't know what to do with this one.

I see myself in the students I work with who were
homeless or have deported family.

And the only words that seem to find
their way out are: Si Se Puede.

estuDiosa

Born of the sun and the moon.
Curiosa y estudiosa.

Nourished by the blue rivers and
brown earth.

First to college and future doctora.
From casa to classroom.
Spanglish to English.
Unlearning to learn.

Resilient. Poderosa. Fuerte y Capaz.
Embraced by the roaring earth.
Sharing knowledge and research
between the rigid mountains and
unspoiled valleys.

Soy una Diosa.

When

When do you know you've "made it"?
When you finally have your own bed or your own
room and don't have to share it?

When do you know you've made it?
When you move out of the hood, and into a
community where you feel safe walking at night?

When do you know you've made it?
When you have college degrees and a car to call your
own?

When do you know you've made it?
When you can take spontaneous trips? Or go to the
movies and have dinner with a friend? Or buy each
of your family members a Christmas gift?

When do you know you've made it?
.
.
.
When you can afford it...

In-between

You know there's something there,
but others don't believe you.
Being bi-, fluid or anything in-between
has felt like having an imaginary friend.
You have to keep trying to convince them and
sometimes even yourself- that it's real
and not just a phase.
You're asked to choose one over the other,
because you can't possibly be both.
But the in-between does exist.
In the Muxes of Oaxaca, Mexico.
In the sistergirls/brotherboys in
Aboriginal, Australia.
In Hijras within Muslim and Hindu cultures in India.
In Fa'afafines from Samoa and New Zealand.
In Warias living in Indonesia.
In the two-spirit people across the
First Nations of North America.
I am made up of everyone and
everything that came before me.
And the in-between exists in me.

They- Them-Theirs

An ode to my friends who want to be seen and heard.

Watch them as they transform our world.

Theirs is the sun, the moon, the air.
They just want to be treated fair.
Pink and blue, or rainbow wear.
Shimmering radiant lustrous hair.
Standing there fearless and bare.
Please try to care.

They're one of a kind, exceptional and rare.

Fight, Flight or Freeze

When they asked me why I didn't leave?
I answered: I don't know.

When he stuck his cold clammy hands down my
pants inside the bar-
I didn't leave.

When my hotel room had bugs
crawling on the walls- I didn't leave.

When he called me fat on a date- I didn't leave.

When he said he didn't want to date me-
I didn't leave.

When he cheated on me- I didn't leave.

When my boss called me a bitch - I didn't leave.

When my dad verbally abused my mom for years-
She didn't leave.

When my grandpa beat my pregnant grandmother's
belly- She didn't leave.

When my aunt's boyfriend slapped her face, left it
purple and red- She didn't leave.

When my aunt cut up all of her son's clothes into tiny
pieces- He didn't leave.

When my uncle beat my aunt with a wooden paddle-
She didn't leave.

When my uncles robbed my grandma's home, stole
every Christmas gift under the tree, took the pots
and pans, radio and tv- We didn't leave.

No one leaves in my family.
We don't know how to.

That's why I didn't leave.

Within Us

Within us pain.
Loss.
Grief.
Within us strength.
Growth.
Power.
Within us joy.
Love.
A new day.

Clouds of Trauma

There's a cloud. A fog, living in my head.
It rains. It pours. And I can't move ahead.

I lay quiet and lifeless in bed.
Wondering if I'm dead.

I blink, not even remembering what I read.
But I know it was the most powerful thing
that was said.

Still. There's a cloud. A fog. Living in my head.

Anxiety

Racing heart and heavy chest.
Memories lingering like a pest.
Never getting any rest.
Because my body remembers
something I don't.
Something I won't.
Tears come out.
Without a doubt.
Unwanted guests
at my door
wanting more.

Forgetful

My mind, a white blanket.
Fluffy, soft and safe.

Where there was pain.

A shower of endorphins.
Make me go tingly then numb.
Forgetful I've become.

Questions swirl over and over
again.
Was that me?
I don't remember who I set out to
be.

Forgetful I am and I can't see.
Thankful for my body high guiding
me into the sky, a fog.

Clouds, fluffy, soft and safe.

The Man Who Loved Me First

Jailed at 34.
A hug, a kiss.
He was someone I'd always miss.
A laugh and a yell.
A grin and a fight.
Loved and adored.
Gunned down at 44.
May he finally know peace.
A hug, a kiss.
He is someone I'll always miss.

Gone

I reach for you but you're gone.
I fall and scrape my knees.
Is love supposed to feel this way?
Mejor quedatelo. I don't want it.
I prefer you gone.
I don't need band aids...anymore.

Homeless

I was welcomed into a little blue house.
And slept on a couch big enough for a
mouse.

I knew I didn't belong.

And didn't even get to stay that long.
The little blue house told me to stay
away. "In here you can't lay."

And on my way I went again.
Searching for a new place on that very
same day.

Assimilation

I crush my bones and shave off limbs to fit into the
cookie cutter shape, but I always spill out.
I trim my tongue to pronounce my name more
American, but they still have trouble saying it.
I bleach my skin white and mash all the
wild coils out of my head.
I plunge a stopper down my throat
to prevent me from:
eating, speaking, breathing different.
I gasp for normal, as if it was air.
I bite my nails, nervous to be seen.
But I let the underground railroad
in my belly lead me to freedom.
Memories of Mexico and family traditions sing
themselves out of the dark liberating my spirit and
keeping my culture alive.
I tell myself: be brave and embrace the scars left on your
body because they tell a story that is hard to hear.
And when you survive death, let your story breathe
courage into others.
Let your existence BE resistance.
Stay strong. Stay alive. Stay you.

Beautiful Brown Body

You're a glowing reminder of what love looks like on
a warm summer day.
But you hate your skin...
Try to wash the brown away as if it were dirt.
That stone in your hand, a weapon... used to scrub off
that which makes you, YOU.
Flesh unravels off your body
and you begin to morph into something else.
Trimming and taming your
rebellious Afghan afro into place like
unwanted wild weeds in a garden.
The upkeep of trying to fit in
is costing you your sanity.
But here I am, falling for every inch of dark skin that
is not enough for you, and is enough for me.

You are enough.
You are Enough.
YOU are ENOUGH.

A Love Letter to my Lonjas

There is a strength in your body.
Gathering in the middle.
Popping under the edges of your bra strap and over
the sides of your waistband.
It's time to reclaim the power living in your rolls.
There are slivers of courage from your native
American. Jewish. Irish. Nigerian. Congolese.
And Guinean ancestors.
You may not know their names, but they know yours.
Loving yourself means you have the power to heal
generations after you.
Loving yourself is how you challenge traditional,
western, and colonial beauty standards. Loving
yourself is an act of resistance, defiance & strength.
Set aside the shame and guilt
revolving around food and your body.
You deserve better. Mira tus lonjitas llenas de amor.
Enjoy the home-made birria served on your plate by
your mom and abuelita. Love is steaming from the
stew. And when they ask
if you want another tortilla, say yes!
Chinga la dieta y chingate otro taco.

A Love Letter to my Longing

Ámate

Ámate hoy.
Porque al amanecer ya sera muy tarde.
Eres imperfecta, y eso te hace única.
Deja que tus cejas florezcan sobre tus ojos.
Deja que tu cabello chino, ondulado o lacio, en su
naturaleza, encuentre tu cuello como dos amistades
que se reencuentran con mucho cariño.
Deja que los bellos sobre tus piernas se besen.
Abandona la imagen de ser perfecta. No existe.
Eres una obra de arte,
como los colores de una nuevo amanecer.
Enfócate mejor en cómo tu cuerpo te arma
como un rompecabezas sobre la mesa.
No todos lograran ver lo que serás algun día.
Pero el tú, el tú real, vendrá pronto.
Ten paciencia.
Ámate.
Tú, eres lo unico que necesitaras en esta vida.
Ámate.

The Healing

My body knows it's the weekend.

In my belly hunger pains surface aching to move,
dance and heal to the rhythms that awaken a wild-
untamed- raw
and unpredictable side of me.

There is strength in my unfiltered body giving zero
f**** about what people may think of me as I sweat off
my make-up and my hair frizzes. I belong to myself.

That is my addiction and healing.

Rebirth

I don't have any room for babies in my belly because
I'm nurturing the forgotten child within.

Abandoned. Ignored. Erased.

I've become my own mother wrapping my arms
firmly around my waist, speaking these words
sofly: 'you will be safe again'.

My stomach rumbles,
empty and hungry without a father.

I disappear again into the night.
Sink beneath a shadow, where I can't breathe.

Depression has lodged itself like an anchor
down my throat ready to dock...
choking on the same thought over and over.

Be Calm. Quiet. Listen.

The thumps in my chest are chanting, singing, yelling out a desperate prayer to be healed.

I take what shaking breath I have left and navigate the streams up my veins to find my heart. Beating. Blessed with brief moments of relief as I learn to shed off the toxic cargo along the way called: negative self-talk, self-sabotage, and insecure attachments.

Love greets me like a life-raft, unexpected, where I finally find peace.

Committed to myself once again.

Nursing joy and strength back into my body. Learning that I am everything I will ever need.

Prompts to Help You Process…

(Write and heal one day at a time)

Write a love letter to yourself.

Write a poem about a dream you had. If you need inspiration, google what the dream meant and then reflect on it.

Write 5 sentences and start with: "Every day…" and see what memories come out. (What's something you do every day?)

Every day…

Every day…

Every day…

Every day…

Every day…

Journal the 3 emotions that come up right now and why those are surfacing for you.

Write about your favorite childhood memory.

Write out a vision statement for yourself (What's your life goal? What are your values?).

Write about an identity you're proud of (Daughter/Son, Immigrant, Parent, First Generation College Student, Non-binary, Queer, Black, Mexican, Artist, Singer, Latinx).

Name three things that make you smile and write down why they make you smile.

Name one emotion and give it a physical body, give it a name, a career, a hobby, give them a story.

Write about your favorite travel destination or your hometown. What do you like about it? What do you miss? Who lives there?

Write a love poem for your child, friend, parent, significant other.

Choose a text in your phone & write a poem about it.

Write a poem that includes the words: pan dulce, piñata, fiesta, flores, familia, & siesta.

Name three things you value (for me, it's story-telling, relationships, & authenticity) and develop a mission statement for yourself.

Write down 10 ways you can be an ally to marginalized people. Be specific, think of: race, gender, class, nationality etc. DM me on IG: @PinkChicanaPoet if you need help!

Write down an apology to yourself or someone who you need to make amends with.

Create your own fairy-tale with you as the main character.

Reflect on your experiences now and growing up: What did your family or society tell you about the words queer/gay or transgender? What was said or implied or not said? How can you show up in solidarity with these groups of people?

Write a list of 10 questions you have for someone or about something. Maybe there's traditions or things you never talk about?

Write about an experience that made you grow and why it matters to you.

Draw yourself (stick figures are ok) and label 10 nice things you like about YOU. Not just physical traits, but your personality as well. You are more than a body!

Write an ode to about something you love using your gender pronouns (She/Him/Ella/El/They/Elle).

Talk about your parents or caretakers or mentors. What qualities do you value in them and hope to adopt? What type of relationship do you have with them? How has this impacted the relationships you're in?

What's your biggest fear and why? Now, who and what can help you make it less scary?

What empowers/motivates you?

Write down 5 affirmations. Now look in the mirror and recite them to yourself. Put them somewhere visible- the bathroom mirror or fridge door.

Write a poem using at least 5 words from another language (other than your native tongue) about something you love. Get creative, use google or ask a friend!

Write a paragraph manifesting at least 5 goals you envision for yourself in the future.

Take a deep breath and write down all the insecurities and burdens weighing you down. Crumple them up and let them go.

No writing prompt today. Do something that makes you smile. Then, make someone else smile.

Pink Chicana Poet's Coloring Book

De Colores

Pink Chicana Poet

Pink Chicana Poet

QUEER PEOPLE IN STRAIGHT RELATIONSHIPS ARE STILL **QUEER**

Pink Chicana Poet

PINK CHICANA POET

112

LEARN TO REST, NOT TO QUIT.

my culture
& gender
are gifts
to eradicate
injustice in
this world

PINK CHICANA POF

116

Growing into a badass version of my self

Pink Chicano Poet

Menos
bla bla bla
y más
glu glu glu

PINK CHICANA POET

It is confidence in our mind, body & spirit that allows us to feel sexy. Be sexy for you.

PINK CHICANA POET

GIRLS JUST WANNA HAVE FUNDAMENTAL RIGHTS

Pink Chicana Poet

STAY CHINGONA

Pink Chicano Poet

Mujer
self-care is
how you
take your
power
back

PINK CHICANA POET

124

Take Life
One SIP
at a Time

PINK CHICANA POET

About the Author

Sinai Cota is a Mexican-American, Latinx/Chicana poet from San Diego, CA. She grew up in the small community of Barrio Logan and has roots extending into Mexico. She is the proud daughter of immigrants, a first generation college student with a Bachelor's in Religious Studies from San Diego State University, a Masters in Education Leadership Studies from The University of San Diego. She currently works as an educator and is enrolled in the Joint Doctoral Program in Education with UC San Diego and Cal State San Marcos University.

In her spare time, Sinai spends it serving her community as a core member of the SD LGBTQ Latinx Coalition and also coordinates The Nancy Brusch Memorial Scholarship with Urban Life, a nonprofit that supports urban youth leaders through jobs, tutoring, and mentorship.

Sinai has had a long-standing relationship with storytelling and writing. The first books she ever wrote were in the 2nd and 3rd grades and were inspired by novelas. She is now the self-published author of *Pink Poems Tan Thoughts* and co-author of *Mujeres in Movement. Pan Dulce for the Latinx Soul,* was born out of a deep desire to share the Latinx experience, from someone who grew up straddling two countries. Sinai calls for us to have hard conversations about taboo topics in the Latinx culture and in our society. We must learn to unlearn and become better advocates not just for ourselves, but for our families, and communities across the world. We face the same problems and our survival depends on our unity.

If you have questions about these topics, or any poems, feel free to DM Sinai on *Instagram at*: *@PinkChicanaPoet* where she promotes messages of community, self-care & self-love.

Please don't forget to leave a review on Amazon (you don't need an account) on GoodReads.com, or share a selfie with a review on social media to help raise awareness of this book's goal to raise funds for college scholarships!

Gracias!!!

Made in the USA
Las Vegas, NV
07 September 2021